On Love

On Love

A SELECTION OF FAMOUS
LOVE POEMS & LOVE LETTERS

WORTH
PRESS

This edition prepared and designed by Worth Press Ltd;
selection by Rosemary Gray; typeset by Antony Gray;
for Monti Publishing & More, Canada

Copyright © Worth Press Ltd 2014

ISBN 978 1 84931 083 3

Cover design by Paul Kawai, Indigo Books & Music Inc.
Printed and bound in Canada

Contents

FAMOUS LOVE POEMS

FAMOUS LOVE LETTERS

A FAMOUS LOVE LETTER FROM FICTION

A LOVER'S REPROACH

Famous
Love
Poems

Sonnet 43

How do I love thee? Let me count the ways.
I love thee to the depth and breadth and height
My soul can reach, when feeling out of sight
For the ends of being and ideal grace.
I love thee to the level of every day's
Most quiet need, by sun and candlelight.
I love thee freely, as men strive for right;
I love thee purely, as they turn from praise.
I love thee with the passion put to use
In my old griefs, and with my childhood's faith.
I love thee with a love I seemed to lose
With my lost saints. I love thee with the breath,
Smiles, tears, of all my life! and, if God choose,
I shall but love thee better after death.

ELIZABETH BARRETT BROWNING

from *Sonnets from the Portuguese*

Sonnet 14

If thou must love me, let it be for nought
Except for love's sake only. Do not say
'I love her for her smile . . . her look . . . her way
Of speaking gently, . . . for a trick of thought
That falls in well with mine, and certes brought
A sense of pleasant ease on such a day' –
For these things in themselves, Belovèd, may
Be changed, or change for thee – and love, so
    wrought,
May be unwrought so. Neither love me for
Thine own dear pity's wiping my cheeks dry –
A creature might forget to weep, who bore
Thy comfort long, and lose thy love thereby!
But love me for love's sake, that evermore
Thou mayst love on, through love's eternity.

ELIZABETH BARRETT BROWNING

'Sonnet 14' from *Sonnets from the Portuguese*

Sonnet 23

Is it indeed so? If I lay here dead,
Wouldst thou miss any life in losing mine?
And would the sun for thee more coldly shine
Because of grave-damps falling round my head?
I marvelled, my Belovèd, when I read
Thy thought so in the letter. I am thine –
But . . . *so* much to thee? Can I pour thy wine
While my hands tremble? Then my soul, instead
Of dreams of death, resumes life's lower range.
Then love me, Love! look on me . . . breathe on me!
As brighter ladies do not count it strange,
For love, to give up acres and degree,
I yield the grave for thy sake, and exchange
My near sweet view of Heaven, for earth with thee!

ELIZABETH BARRETT BROWNING

from *Sonnets from the Portuguese*

Love's Secret

Never seek to tell thy love,
Love that never told can be;
For the gentle wind does move

Silently, invisibly.
I told my love,
I told my love,
I told her all my heart;
Trembling, cold, in ghastly fears,
Ah! she did depart!

Soon as she was gone from me,
A traveller came by,
Silently, invisibly,
He took her with a sigh.

WILLIAM BLAKE

The Garden of Love

I went to the Garden of Love,
And saw what I never had seen:
A chapel was built in the midst,
Where I used to play on the green.

And the gates of this chapel were shut,
And 'Thou shalt not' writ over the door;
So I turn'd to the Garden of Love
That so many sweet flowers bore;

And I saw it was filled with graves,
And tombstones where flowers should be;
And priests in black gowns were walking
                          their rounds,
And binding with briars my joys and desires.

WILLIAM BLAKE

I See You, Juliet

I see you, Juliet, still, with your straw hat
Loaded with vines, and with your dear pale face,
On which those thirty years so lightly sat,
And the white outline of your muslin dress.
You wore a litte fichu trimmed with lace
And crossed in the front, as was the fashion then,
Bound at your waist with a broad band or sash,
All white and fresh and virginally plain.
There was a sound of shouting far away
Down in the valley, as they called to us,
And you, with hands clasped seeming still to pray
Patience of fate, stood listening to me thus
With heaving bosom. There a rose lay curled.
It was the reddest rose in all the world.

WILFRED BLUNT

The Night Has a Thousand Eyes

The night has a thousand eyes,
    And the day but one;
Yet the light of the bright world dies
    With the dying sun.

The mind has a thousand eyes,
    And the heart but one;
Yet the light of a whole life dies,
    When love is done.

FRANCIS WILLIAM BOURDILLON

I Will Not Let Thee Go

I will not let thee go.
Ends all our month-long love in this?
  Can it be summed up so,
  Quit in a single kiss?
I will not let thee go.

I will not let thee go.
If thy words' breath could scare
                thy deeds,
  As the soft south can blow
  And toss the feathered seeds,
  Then might I let thee go.

I will not let thee go.
Had not the great sun seen, I might;
  Or were he reckoned slow
  To bring the false to light,
  Then might I let thee go.

I will not let thee go.
The stars that crowd the summer skies
  Have watched us so below
  With all their million eyes,
  I dare not let thee go.

I will not let thee go.
Have we chid the changeful moon,
  Now rising late, and now
  Because she set too soon,
  And shall I let thee go?

I will not let thee go.
Have not the young flowers been content,
    Plucked ere their buds could blow,
    To seal our sacrament?
    I cannot let thee go.

I will not let thee go.
I hold thee by too many bands:
    Thou sayest farewell, and lo!
    I have thee by the hands,
    And will not let thee go.

ROBERT BRIDGES

Remembrance

Cold in the earth – and the deep snow piled
                                    above thee,
Far, far, removed, cold in the dreary grave!
Have I forgot, my only Love, to love thee,
Severed at last by Time's all-severing wave?

Now, when alone, do my thoughts no longer hover
Over the mountains, on that northern shore,
Resting their wings where heath and fern-
                            leaves cover
Thy noble heart for ever, ever more?

Cold in the earth – and fifteen wild Decembers,
From those brown hills, have melted into spring:
Faithful, indeed, is the spirit that remembers
After such years of change and suffering!

Sweet Love of youth, forgive, if I forget thee,
While the world's tide is bearing me along;
Other desires and other hopes beset me,
Hopes which obscure, but cannot do thee wrong!

No later light has lightened up my heaven,
No second morn has ever shone for me;
All my life's bliss from thy dear life was given,
All my life's bliss is in the grave with thee.

But, when the days of golden dreams had
                                    perished,
And even Despair was powerless to destroy;
Then did I learn how existence could be
                                    cherished,
Strengthened, and fed without the aid of joy.

Then did I check the tears of useless passion –
Weaned my young soul from yearning
                          after thine;
Sternly denied its burning wish to hasten
Down to that tomb already more than mine.

And, even yet, I dare not let it languish,
Dare not indulge in memory's rapturous pain;
Once drinking deep of that divinest anguish,
How could I seek the empty world again?

EMILY BRONTË

Love and Friendship

Love is like the wild rose briar,
Friendship like the holly tree –
The holly is dark when the rose briar blooms
But which will bloom most constantly?

The wild rose-briar is sweet in spring,
Its summer blossoms scent the air;
Yet wait till winter comes again
And who will call the wild briar fair?

Then scorn the silly rose wreath now
And deck thee with the holly's sheen,
That when December blights thy brow
He still may leave thy garland green.

EMILY BRONTË

Love

Love is a breach in the walls, a broken gate,
    Where that comes in that shall not go again;
Love sells the proud heart's citadel to Fate.
    They have known shame, who love unloved.
                                    Even then
When two mouths, thirsty each for each,
                            find slaking,
    And agony's forgot, and hushed the crying
Of credulous hearts, in heaven – such are but taking
    Their own poor dreams within their arms,
                            and lying
Each in his lonely night, each with a ghost.
    Some share that night. But they know,
                        love grows colder,
Grows false and dull, that was sweet lies at most.
    Astonishment is no more in hand or shoulder,
But darkens, and dies out from kiss to kiss.
All this is love; and all love is but this.

RUPERT BROOKE

25

The Hill

Breathless, we flung us on the windy hill,
   Laughed in the sun, and kissed the lovely grass.
   You said, 'Through glory and ecstasy we pass;
Wind, sun, and earth remain, the birds sing still,
When we are old, are old . . .' 'And when we die
   All's over that is ours; and life burns on
Through other lovers, other lips,' said I,
   'Heart of my heart, our heaven is now, is won!'

'We are earth's best, that learnt her lesson here.
   Life is our cry. We have kept the faith!' we said;
   'We shall go down with unreluctant tread
Rose-crowned into the darkness!' . . . Proud we were,
And laughed, that had such brave true things to say.
– And then you suddenly cried, and turned away.

RUPERT BROOKE

26

Meeting at Night

The grey sea and the long black land;
And the yellow half-moon large and low;
And the startled little waves that leap
In fiery ringlets from their sleep,
As I gain the cove with pushing prow,
And quench its speed i' the slushy sand.

Then a mile of warm sea-scented beach;
Three fields to cross till a farm appears;
A tap at the pane, the quick sharp scratch
And blue spurt of a lighted match,
And a voice less loud, thro' its joys and fears,
Than the two hearts beating each to each!

ROBERT BROWNING

A Woman's Last Word

Let's contend no more, Love,
　　Strive nor weep:
All be as before, Love,
　　– Only sleep!

What so wild as words are?
　　I and thou
In debate, as birds are,
　　Hawk on bough!

See the creature stalking
　　While we speak!
Hush and hide the talking,
　　Cheek on cheek!

What so false as truth is,
　　False to thee?
Where the serpent's tooth is
　　Shun the tree –

Where the apple reddens
　　Never pry –
Lest we lose our Edens,
　　Eve and I.

Be a god and hold me
　　With a charm!
Be a man and fold me
　　With thine arm!

Teach me, only teach, Love!
  As I ought
I will speak thy speech, Love,
  Think thy thought –

Meet, if thou require it,
  Both demands,
Laying flesh and spirit
  In thy hands.

That shall be tomorrow
  Not tonight:
I must bury sorrow
  Out of sight:

– Must a little weep, Love,
  (Foolish me!)
And so fall asleep, Love,
  Loved by thee.

ROBERT BROWNING

A Light Woman

So far as our story approaches the end,
　　Which do you pity the most of us three? –
My friend, or the mistress of my friend
　　With her wanton eyes, or me?

My friend was already too good to lose,
　　And seemed in the way of improvement yet,
When she crossed his path with her hunting-noose
　　And over him drew her net.

When I saw him tangled in her toils,
　　A shame, said I, if she adds just him
To her nine-and-ninety other spoils,
　　The hundredth for a whim!

And before my friend be wholly hers,
　　How easy to prove to him, I said,
An eagle's the game her pride prefers,
　　Though she snaps at a wren instead!

So, I gave her eyes my own eyes to take,
　　My hand sought hers as in earnest need,
And round she turned for my noble sake,
　　And gave me herself indeed.

The eagle am I, with my fame in the world,
　　The wren is he, with his maiden face.
– You look away and your lip is curled?
　　Patience, a moment's space!

For see, my friend goes shaking and white;
    He eyes me as the basilisk:
I have turned, it appears, his day to night,
    Eclipsing his sun's disk.

And I did it, he thinks, as a very thief:
    'Though I love her' – that, he comprehends –
'One should master one's passions,' (love, in chief)
    'And be loyal to one's friends!'

And she – she lies in my hand as tame
    As a pear late basking over a wall;
Just a touch to try and off it came;
    'Tis mine – can I let it fall?

With no mind to eat it, that's the worst!
    Were it thrown in the road, would the case assist?
'Twas quenching a dozen blue-flies' thirst
    When I gave its stalk a twist.

And I – what I seem to my friend, you see:
    What I soon shall seem to his love, you guess:
What I seem to myself, do you ask of me?
    No hero, I confess.

'Tis an awkward thing to play with souls,
    And matter enough to save one's own:
Yet think of my friend, and the burning coals
    He played with for bits of stone!

One likes to show the truth for the truth;
    That the woman was light is very true:
But suppose she says – Never mind that youth!
    What wrong have I done to you?

Well, anyhow, here the story stays,
    So far at least as I understand;
And, Robert Browning, you writer of plays,
    Here's a subject made to your hand!

ROBERT BROWNING

Never the Time and the Place

Never the time and the place
    And the loved one all together!
This path – how soft to pace!
    This May – what magic weather!
Where is the loved one's face?
In a dream that loved one's face meets mine,
    But the house is narrow, the place is bleak
Where, outside, rain and wind combine
    With a furtive ear, if I strive to speak,
    With a hostile eye at my flushing cheek,
With a malice that marks each word, each sign!
O enemy sly and serpentine,
    Uncoil thee from the waking man!
        Do I hold the past
        Thus firm and fast
    Yet doubt if the future hold I can?
This path so soft to pace shall lead
Thro' the magic of May to herself indeed!
Or narrow if needs the house must be,
Outside are the storms and strangers: we –
Oh, close, safe, warm sleep I and she –
I and she!

ROBERT BROWNING

My Love is Like a Red Red Rose

My love is like a red red rose
　That's newly sprung in June:
My love is like the melodie
　That's sweetly play'd in tune.

So fair art thou, my bonnie lass,
　So deep in love am I:
And I will love thee still, my dear,
　Till a' the seas gang dry.

Till a' the seas gang dry, my dear,
　And the rocks melt wi' the sun:
And I will love thee still, my dear,
　While the sands o' life shall run.

And fare thee weel, my only love,
　And fare thee weel awhile!
And I will come again, my love,
　Tho' it were ten thousand mile.

ROBERT BURNS

Delia

Fair the face of orient day,
Fair the tints of op'ning rose;
But fairer still my Delia dawns,
More lovely far her beauty blows.

Sweet the lark's wild-warbled lay,
Sweet the tinkling rill to hear;
But, Delia, more delightful still,
Steal thine accents on mine ear.

The flower-enamour'd busy bee
The rosy banquet loves to sip;
Sweet the streamlet's limpid lapse
To the sun-brown'd Arab's lip;

But, Delia, on thy balmy lips
Let me, no vagrant insect, rove!
O let me steal one liquid kiss!
For Oh! my soul is parch'd with love!

ROBERT BURNS

Jockey's Ta'en the Parting Kiss

Jockey's ta'en the parting kiss,
   O'er the mountains he is gane;
And with him is a' my bliss,
   Nought but griefs with me remain.

Spare my luve, ye winds that blaw,
   Plashy sleets and beating rain!
Spare my luve, thou feathery snaw,
   Drifting o'er the frozen plain!

When the shades of evening creep
   O'er the day's fair, gladsome ee,
Sound and safely may he sleep,
   Sweetly blithe his waukening be!

He will think on her he loves,
   Fondly he'll repeat her name;
For where'er he distant roves,
   Jockey's heart is still the same.

ROBERT BURNS

She Walks in Beauty

She walks in beauty, like the night
  Of cloudless climes and starry skies;
And all that's best of dark and bright
  Meet in her aspect and her eyes:
Thus mellowed to that tender light
  Which heaven to gaudy day denies.

One shade the more, one ray the less,
  Had half impaired the nameless grace,
Which waves in every raven tress,
  Or softly lightens o'er her face;
Where thoughts serenely sweet express,
  How pure, how dear their dwelling-place.

And on the cheek, and o'er that brow,
  So soft, so calm, yet eloquent,
The smiles that win, the tints that glow,
  But tell of days in goodness spent,
A mind at peace with all below,
  A heart whose love is innocent!

GEORGE GORDON, LORD BYRON

When We Two Parted

When we two parted
In silence and tears,
Half broken-hearted,
To sever for years,
Pale grew thy cheek and cold,
Colder thy kiss;
Truly that hour foretold
Sorrow to this!

The dew of the morning
Sunk chill on my brow;
It felt like the warning
Of what I feel now.
Thy vows are all broken,
And light is thy fame:
I hear thy name spoken
And share in its shame.
They name thee before me,
A knell to mine ear;
A shudder comes o'er me –
Why wert thou so dear?
They know not I knew thee
Who knew thee too well:
Long, long shall I rue thee
Too deeply to tell.

In secret we met:
In silence I grieve
That thy heart could forget,

Thy spirit deceive.
If I should meet thee
After long years,
How should I greet thee? –
With silence and tears.

GEORGE GORDON, LORD BYRON

First Love

I ne'er was struck before that hour,
   With love so sudden and so sweet.
Her face it bloomed like a sweet flower,
   And stole my heart away complete.
My face turned pale, a deadly pale,
   My legs refused to walk away,
And when she looked what could I ail,
   My life and all seemed turned to clay.

And then my blood rushed to my face,
   And took my eyesight quite away.
The trees and bushes round the place,
   Seemed midnight at noonday.
I could not see a single thing,
   Words from my eyes did start.
They spoke as chords do from the string,
   And blood burnt round my heart.

Are flowers the winter's choice?
   Is love's bed always snow?
She seemed to hear my silent voice,
   Not love's appeals to know.
I never saw so sweet a face
   As that I stood before.
My heart has left its dwelling place
   And can return no more.

JOHN CLARE

Wild Nights

Wild nights! Wild nights!
Were I with thee,
Wild nights should be
Our luxury!

Futile the winds
To a heart in port –
Done with the compass,
Done with the chart.

Rowing in Eden!
Ah! the sea!
Might I but moor
Tonight in thee!

EMILY DICKINSON

The Outlet

My river runs to thee:
Blue sea, wilt welcome me?

My river waits reply.
Oh sea, look graciously!

I'll fetch thee brooks
From spotted nooks –

Say, sea,
Take me!

EMILY DICKINSON

The Master

He fumbles at your spirit
   As players at the keys
Before they drop full music on;
   He stuns you by degrees,

Prepares your brittle substance
   For the ethereal blow,
By fainter hammers, further heard,
   Then nearer, then so slow

Your breath has time to straighten,
   Your brain to bubble cool –
Deals one imperial thunderbolt
   That scalps your naked soul.

EMILY DICKINSON

Love

Love is anterior to life,
 Posterior to death,
Initial of creation, and
 The exponent of breath.

EMILY DICKINSON

We Outgrow Love Like Other Things

We outgrow love like other things
 And put it in the drawer,
Till it an antique fashion shows
 Like costumes grandsires wore.

EMILY DICKINSON

Longing

I envy seas whereon he rides,
　I envy spokes of wheels
Of chariots that him convey,
　I envy speechless hills

That gaze upon his journey;
　How easy all can see
What is forbidden utterly
　As heaven, unto me!

I envy nests of sparrows
　That dot his distant eaves,
The wealthy fly upon his pane,
　The happy, happy leaves

That just abroad his window
　Have summer's leave to be,
The earrings of Pizarro
　Could not obtain for me.

I envy light that wakes him,
　And bells that boldly ring
To tell him it is noon abroad –
　Myself his noon could bring,

Yet interdict my blossom
　And abrogate my bee,
Lest noon in everlasting night
　Drop Gabriel and me.

EMILY DICKINSON

The Lost Jewel

I held a jewel in my fingers
And went to sleep.
The day was warm, and winds were prosy;
I said: ' 'Twill keep.'

I woke and chid my honest fingers –
The gem was gone;
And now an amethyst remembrance
Is all I own.

EMILY DICKINSON

Apotheosis

Come slowly, Eden!
Lips unused to thee,
Bashful, sip thy jasmines,
As the fainting bee,

Reaching late his flower,
Round her chamber hums,
Counts his nectars – enters,
And is lost in balms!

EMILY DICKINSON

An Epithalamion

or Marriage song on the Lady Elizabeth and Count
Palatine being married on St Valentines Day.

1

Haile Bishop Valentine, whose day this is,
  All the Aire is thy Diocis,
  And all the chirping Choristers
And other birds are thy Parishioners,
  Thou marryest every yeare
The Lirique Larke, and the grave whispering Dove,
The Sparrow that neglects his life for love,
The household Bird, with the red stomacher,
  Thou mak'st the blackbird speed as soone,
As doth the Goldfinch, or the Halcyon;
The husband cocke lookes out, and straight is sped,
And meets his wife, which brings her feather-bed.
This day more cheerfully then ever shine,
This day, which might enflame thyself,
      Old Valentine.

2

Till now, Thou warmd'st with multiplying loves
  Two larkes, two sparrowes, or two Doves,
  All that is nothing unto this,
For thou this day couplest two Phœnixes;
  Thou mak'st a Taper see
What the sunne never saw, and what the Arke
(Which was of foules, and beasts, the cage,
      and park,)

48

Did not containe, one bed containes, through Thee,
>Two Phœnixes, whose joyned breasts
Are unto one another mutuall nests,
Where motion kindles such fires, as shall give
Yong Phœnixes, and yet the old shall live.
Whose love and courage never shall decline,
But make the whole year through, thy day,
>>O Valentine.

3

Up then faire Phœnix Bride, frustrate the Sunne,
>Thy selfe from thine affection
>Takest warmth enough, and from thine eye
All lesser birds will take their Jollitie.
>Up, up, faire Bride, and call,
Thy starres, from out their severall boxes, take
Thy Rubies, Pearles, and Diamonds forth, and make
Thy selfe a constellation, of them All,
>And by their blazing, signifie,
That a Great Princess falls, but doth not die;
Bee thou a new starre, that to us portends
Ends of much wonder; And be Thou those ends.
Since thou dost this day in new glory shine,
May all men date Records, from this thy Valentine.

4

Come forth, come forth, and as one glorious flame
>Meeting Another, growes the same,
>So meet thy Fredericke, and so
To an unseparable union growe.
>Since separation
Falls not on such things as are infinite,

49

Nor things which are but one, can disunite,
You'are twice inseparable, great, and one;
      Goe then to where the Bishop staies,
To make you one, his way, which divers waies
Must be effected; and when all is past,
And that you'are one, by hearts and hands
                     made fast,
You two have one way left, your selves to'entwine,
Besides this Bishops knot, or Bishop Valentine.

5

But oh, what ailes the Sunne, that here he staies,
      Longer to day, then other daies?
      Staies he new light from these to get?
And finding here such store, is loth to get?
      And why doe you two walke,
So slowly pac'd in this procession?
Is all your care but to be look'd upon,
And be to others spectacle, and talke?
      The feast, with gluttonous delaies,
Is eaten, and too long their meat they praise,
The masquers come too late, and'I thinke, will stay,
Like Fairies, till the Cock crow them away.
Alas, did not Antiquity assigne
A night, as well as day, to thee, O Valentine?

6

They did, and night is come; and yet wee see
      Formalities retarding thee.
      What meane these Ladies, which (as though
They were to take a clock in peeces,) goe
      So nicely about the Bride;

A Bride, before a good night could be said,
Should vanish from her cloathes, into her bed,
As Soules from bodies steale, and are not spy'd.
      But now she is laid; What though shee bee?
Yet there are more delayes, For, where is he?
He comes, and passes through Spheare after Spheare,
First her sheetes, then her Armes, then anywhere.
Let not this day, then, but this night be thine,
Thy day was but the eve to this, O Valentine.

7

Here lyes a shee Sunne, and a hee Moone here,
      She gives the best light to his Spheare,
      Or each is both, and all, and so
They unto one another nothing owe,
      And yet they doe, but are
So just and rich in that coyne which they pay,
That neither would, nor needs forbeare, nor stay;
Neither desires to be spar'd, nor to spare,
      They quickly pay their debt, and then
Take no acquittances, but pay again;
They pay, they give, they lend, and so let fall
No such occasion to be liberall.
More truth, more courage in these two do shine,
Then all thy turtles have, and sparrows, Valentine.

8

And by this act of these two Phœnixes
      Nature againe restored is,
      For since these two are two no more,

Ther's but one Phœnix still, as was before.
      Rest now at last, and wee
As Satyres watch the Sunnes uprise, will stay
Waiting, when your eyes opened, let out day,
Onely desir'd, because your face wee see;
      Others neare you shall whispering speake,
And wagers lay, at which side day will breake,
And win by'observing, then, whose hand it is
That opens first a curtaine, hers or his;
This will be tryed tomorrow after nine,
Till which houre wee thy day enlarge, O Valentine.

JOHN DONNE

The Good-Morrow

I wonder by my troth, what thou, and I
Did, till we lov'd? were we not wean'd till then?
But suck'd on countrey pleasures, childishly?
Or snorted we in the seaven sleepers den?
T'was so; But this, all pleasures fancies bee.
If ever any beauty I did see,
Which I desir'd, and got, t'was but a dreame
                              of thee.

And now good morrow to our waking soules,
Which watch not one another out of feare;
For love, all love of other sights controules,
And makes one little roome, an every where.
Let sea-discoverers to new worlds have gone,
Let Maps to other, worlds on worlds have showne,
Let us possesse one world, each hath one,
                              and is one.

My face in thine eye, thine in mine appeares,
And true plain hearts doe in the faces rest,
Where can we finde two better hemispheares
Without sharpe North, without declining West?
What ever dyes, was not mixt equally;
If our two loves be one, or, thou and I
Love so alike, that none doe slacken, none can die.

JOHN DONNE

The Sunne Rising

Busie old foole, unruly Sunne,
    Why dost thou thus,
Through windowes, and through curtaines
                   call on us?
Must to thy motions lovers seasons run?
    Sawcy pedantique wretch, goe chide
    Late schoole boyes, and sowre prentices,
  Goe tell Court-huntsmen, that the King will ride,
  Call countrey ants to harvest offices;
Love, all alike, no season knowes, nor clyme,
Nor houres, dayes, moneths, which are the
               rags of time.

    Thy beames, so reverend, and strong
    Why shouldst thou thinke?
I could eclipse and cloud them with a winke,
But that I would not lose her sight so long:
    If her eyes have not blinded thine,
    Looke, and to morrow late, tell mee,
  Whether both the'India's of spice and Myne
  Be where thou leftst them, or lie here with mee.
Aske for those Kings whom thou saw'st yesterday,
And thou shalt heare, All here in one bed lay.

    She'is all States, and all Princes, I,
    Nothing else is.
Princes doe but play us; compar'd to this,

All honor's mimique; All wealth alchimie.
   Thou sunne art halfe as happy'as wee,
   In that the world's contracted thus;
  Thine age askes ease, and since thy duties bee
  To warme the world, that's done in warming us.
Shine here to us, and thou art every where;
This bed thy center is, these walls, thy spheare.

         JOHN DONNE

ƒ

The Flea

Marke but this flea, and marke in this,
How little that which thou deny'st me is;
It suck'd me first, and now sucks thee,
And in this flea, our two bloods mingled bee;
Thou know'st that this cannot be said
A sinne, nor shame, nor losse of maidenhead,
   Yet this enjoyes before it wooe,
   And pamper'd swells with one blood
              made of two,
   And this, alas, is more then wee would doe.

Oh stay, three lives in one flea spare,
Where wee almost, yea more then maryed are,
This flea is you and I, and this
Our mariage bed, and mariage temple is;
Though parents grudge, and you, w'are met,
And cloysterd in these living walls of Jet.
   Though use make you apt to kill mee,
   Let not to that, selfe murder added bee,
   And sacrilege, three sinnes in killing three.

Cruell and sodaine, hast thou since
Purpled thy naile, in blood of innocence?
Wherein could this flea guilty bee,
Except in that drop which it suckt from thee?
Yet thou triumph'st, and saist that thou
Find'st not thy selfe, nor mee the weaker now;

'Tis true, then learne how false, feares bee;
Just so much honor, when thou yeeld'st to mee,
Will wast, as this flea's death tooke life from thee.

JOHN DONNE

Non sum qualis eram bonae sub regno Cynarae

Last night, ah, yesternight, betwixt her lips
                                    and mine
There fell thy shadow, Cynara! thy breath was shed
Upon my soul between the kisses and the wine;
And I was desolate and sick of an old passion,
    Yea, I was desolate and bowed my head:
I have been faithful to thee, Cynara! in my fashion.

All night upon mine heart I felt her warm
                                    heart beat,
Night-long within mine arms in love and
                                    sleep she lay;
Surely the kisses of her bought red mouth
                                    were sweet;
But I was desolate and sick of an old passion,
    When I awoke and found the dawn was grey:
I have been faithful to thee, Cynara! in my fashion.

I have forgot much, Cynara! gone with the wind,
Flung roses, roses riotously with the throng,
Dancing, to put thy pale, lost lilies out of mind;
But I was desolate and sick of an old passion,
    Yea, all the time, because the dance was long:
I have been faithful to thee, Cynara! in my fashion.

I cried for madder music and for stronger wine,
But when the feast is finished and the lamps expire,

Then falls thy shadow, Cynara! the night is thine;
And I am desolate and sick of an old passion,
   Yea, hungry for the lips of my desire:
I have been faithful to thee, Cynara! in my fashion.

ERNEST DOWSON

Love One Another

Love one another, but make not a bond of love.
Let it rather be a moving sea between the shores
of your souls.

Fill each other's cup, but drink not from one cup.
Give one another of your bread, but eat not from
the same loaf.

Sing and dance together and be joyous, but let
each one of you be alone,
Even as the strings of a lute are alone though
they quiver with the same music.

Give your hearts, but not into each other's keeping.
For only the hand of life can contain your hearts.

And stand together, yet not too near together.
For the pillars of the temple stand apart.
And the oak tree and the cypress grow not in
each other's shadow.

KHALIL GIBRAN

The Departure Platform

We kissed at the barrier; and passing through
She left me, and moment by moment got
Smaller and smaller, until to my view
      She was but a spot;

A wee white spot of muslin fluff
That down the diminishing platform bore
Through hustling crowds of gentle and rough
      To the carriage door.

Under the lamplight's fitful glowers,
Behind dark groups from far and near,
Whose interests were apart from ours,
      She would disappear,

Then show again, till I ceased to see
That flexible form, that nebulous white;
And she who was more than my life to me
      Had vanished quite.

We have penned new plans since that fair fond day,
And in season she will appear again –
Perhaps in the same soft white array –
      But never as then!

– 'And why, young man, must eternally fly
A joy you'll repeat, if you love her well?'
– O friend, nought happens twice thus; why,
      I cannot tell!

THOMAS HARDY

The Voice

Woman much missed, how you call to me,
                        call to me,
Saying that now you are not as you were
When you had changed from the one who was
                        all to me,
But as at first, when our day was fair.

Can it be you that I hear? Let me view you, then,
Standing as when I drew near to the town
Where you would wait for me: yes, as I knew
                        you then,
Even to the original air-blue gown!

Or is it only the breeze in its listlessness
Travelling across the wet mead to me here,
You being ever dissolved to wan wistlessness,
Heard no more again far or near?

Thus I; faltering forward,
Leaves around me falling,
Wind oozing thin through the thorn from norward,
And the woman calling.

THOMAS HARDY

Because I Liked You Better

Because I liked you better
 Than suits a man to say,
It irked you, and I promised
 To throw the thought away.

To put the world between us
 We parted, stiff and dry;
'Good-bye,' said you, 'forget me.'
 'I will, no fear,' said I.

If here, where clover whitens
 The dead man's knoll, you pass,
And no tall flower to meet you
 Starts in the trefoiled grass,

Halt by the headstone naming
 The heart no longer stirred,
And say the lad that loved you
 Was one that kept his word.

A. E. HOUSMAN

Song to Celia

Drink to me only with thine eyes,
　And I will pledge with mine;
Or leave a kiss but in the cup
　And I'll not look for wine.
The thirst that from thy soul doth rise
　Doth ask a drink divine;
But might I of Jove's nectar sup,
　I would not change for thine.

I sent thee late a rosy wreath,
　Not so much honouring thee
As giving it a hope that there
　It could not withered be;
But thou thereon didst only breathe,
　And sent'st it back to me:
Since when it grows, and smells, I swear,
　Not of itself, but thee!

BEN JONSON

Bright Star

Bright star, would I were steadfast as thou art –
    Not in lone splendour hung aloft the night
And watching, with eternal lids apart,
    Like nature's patient, sleepless Eremite,
The moving waters at their priestlike task
    Of pure ablution round earth's human shores,
Or gazing on the new soft-fallen mask
    Of snow upon the mountains and the moors –
No – yet still steadfast, still unchangeable,
    Pillow'd upon my fair love's ripening breast,
To feel for ever its soft fall and swell,
    Awake for ever in a sweet unrest,
Still, still to hear her tender-taken breath,
And so live ever – or else swoon to death.

JOHN KEATS

La Belle Dame Sans Merci

Ah, what can ail thee, wretched wight,
   Alone and palely loitering;
The sedge is wither'd from the lake,
   And no birds sing.

Ah, what can ail thee, wretched wight,
   So haggard and so woebegone?
The squirrel's granary is full,
   And the harvest's done.

I see a lily on thy brow,
   With anguish moist and fever dew;
And on thy cheek a fading rose
   Fast withereth too.

I met a lady in the meads
   Full beautiful, a faery's child;
Her hair was long, her foot was light,
   And her eyes were wild.

I set her on my pacing steed,
   And nothing else saw all day long;
For sideways would she lean, and sing
   A feary's song.

I made a garland for her head,
   And bracelets too, and fragrant zone;
She look'd at me as she did love,
   And made sweet moan.

She found me roots of relish sweet,
    And honey wild, and manna dew;
And sure in language strange she said,
    I love thee true.

She took me to her elfin grot,
    And there she gaz'd and sighed deep,
And there I shut her wild sad eyes –
    So kiss'd to sleep.

And there we slumber'd on the moss,
    And there I dream'd, ah woe betide,
The latest dream I ever dream'd
    On the cold hillside.

I saw pale kings, and princes too,
    Pale warriors, death-pale were they all;
Who cry'd – 'La belle Dame sans merci
    Hath thee in thrall!'

I saw their starv'd lips in the gloam
    With horrid warning gaped wide,
And I awoke, and found me here
    On the cold hillside.

And this is why I sojourn here
    Alone and palely loitering,
Though the sedge is wither'd from the lake,
    And no birds sing.

JOHN KEATS

Sonnet

The day is gone, and all its sweets are gone!
  Sweet voice, sweet lips, soft hand, and
                  softer breast,
Warm breath, light whisper, tender semi-tone,
  Bright eyes, accomplish'd shape, and
                  lang'rous waist!
Faded the flower and all its budded charms,
  Faded the sight of beauty from my eyes,
Faded the shape of beauty from my arms,
  Faded the voice, warmth, whiteness, paradise –
Vanish'd unseasonably at shut of eve,
  When the dusk holiday – or holinight
Of fragrant-curtain'd love begins to weave
  The woof of darkness thick, for hid delight;
But, as I've read love's missal through today,
He'll let me sleep, seeing I fast and pray.

JOHN KEATS

She Said as Well to Me

She said as well to me: 'Why are you ashamed?
That little bit of your chest that shows between
the gap of your shirt, why cover it up?
Why shouldn't your legs and your good
        strong thighs
be rough and hairy? – I'm glad they are like that.
You are shy, you silly, you silly shy thing.
Men are the shyest creatures, they never will come
out of their covers. Like any snake
slipping into its bed of dead leaves, you hurry
        into your clothes.
And I love you so! Straight and clean and all of a
        piece is the body of a man,
such an instrument, a spade, like a spear, or an oar,
such a joy to me – '
So she laid her hands and pressed them down
        my sides,
so that I began to wonder over myself, and
        what I was.

She said to me: 'What an instrument, your body!
single and perfectly distinct from everything else!
What a tool in the hands of the Lord!
Only God could have brought it to its shape.
It feels as if his handgrasp, wearing you,
had polished you and hollowed you,
hollowed this groove in your sides, grasped you
        under the breasts

and brought you to the very quick of your form,
subtler than an old, soft-worn fiddle-bow.

'When I was a child, I loved my father's riding-
      whip that he used so often.
I loved to handle it, it seemed like a near part
      of him.
So I did his pens, and the jasper seal on his desk.
Something seemed to surge through me when
      I touched them.

'So it is with you, but here
The joy I feel!
God knows what I feel, but it is joy!
Look, you are clean and fine and singled out!
I admire you so, you are beautiful: this clean
sweep of your sides, this firmness, this
      hard mould!
I would die rather than have it injured with
      one scar.
I wish I could grip you like the fist of the Lord,
and have you – '

So she said, and I wondered,
feeling trammelled and hurt.
It did not make me free.

Now I say to her: 'No tool, no instrument, no God!
Don't touch me and appreciate me.
It is an infamy.

You would think twice before you touched a
      weasel on a fence
as it lifts its straight white throat.
Your hand would not be so flig and easy.
Nor the adder we saw asleep with her head on
      her shoulder,
curled up in the sunshine like a princess;
when she lifted her head in delicate, startled
      wonder
you did not stretch forward to caress her
though she looked rarely beautiful
and a miracle as she glided delicately away, with
      such dignity.
And the young bull in the field, with his
      wrinkled, sad face,
you are afraid if he rises to his feet,
though he is all wistful and pathetic, like a
      monolith, arrested, static.

'Is there nothing in me to make you hesitate?
I tell you there is all these.
And why should you overlook them in me? – '

D. H. LAWRENCE

Gloire de Dijon

When she rises in the morning
I linger to watch her;
She spreads the bath-cloth underneath the window
And the sunbeams catch her
Glistening white on the shoulders,
While down her sides the mellow
Golden shadow glows as
She stoops to the sponge, and her swung breasts
Sway like full-blown yellow
Gloire de Dijon roses.

She drips herself with water, and her shoulders
Glisten as silver, they crumple up
Like wet and falling roses, and I listen
For the sluicing of their rain-dishevelled petals.
In the window full of sunlight
Concentrates her golden shadow
Fold on fold, until it glows as
Mellow as the glory roses.

D. H. LAWRENCE

The Taxi

When I go away from you
The world beats dead,
Like a slackened drum.
I call out for you against the jutted stars
And shout into the ridges of the wind.

Streets coming fast,
One after the other,
Wedge you away from me,
And the lamps of the city prick my eyes
So that I can no longer see your face.
Why should I leave you,
To wound myself upon the sharp edges of the night?

AMY LOWELL

The Shepherd to His Love

Come live with me, and be my love,
And we will all the pleasures prove
That hills and valleys, dales and fields,
Woods or steepy mountain yields.

And we will sit upon the rocks,
Seeing the shepherds feed their flocks
By shallow rivers, to whose falls
Melodious birds sing madrigals.

And I will make thee beds of roses,
And a thousand fragrant posies;
A cap of flowers, and a kirtle,
Embroidered all with leaves of myrtle;

A gown made of the finest wool,
Which from our pretty lambs we pull;
Fair lined slippers for the cold,
With buckles of the purest gold;

A belt of straw and ivy buds,
With coral clasps and amber studs:
And if these pleasures may thee move,
Come live with me, and be my love.

The shepherds' swains shall dance and sing
For thy delight each May morning:
If these delights thy mind may move,
Then live with me, and be my love.

CHRISTOPHER MARLOWE

There was an Hour

In our old shipwrecked days there was an hour,
When in the firelight steadily aglow,
Joined slackly, we beheld the red chasm grow
Among the clicking coals. Our library-bower
That eve was left to us: and hushed we sat
As lovers to whom time is whispering.
From sudden-opened doors we heard them sing.
The nodding elders mixed good wine with chat.
Well knew we that life's greatest treasure lay
With us, and of it was our talk. 'Ah, yes!
Love dies!' I said: I never thought it less.
She yearned to me that sentence to unsay.
Then when the fire domed blackening, I found
Her cheek was salt against my kiss, and swift
Up the sharp scale of sobs her breast did lift –
Now am I haunted by that taste! that sound!

GEORGE MEREDITH
from *Modern Love*

Renouncement

I must not think of thee; and, tired yet strong,
I shun the thought that lurks in all delight –
The thought of thee – and in the blue heaven's
                                    height,
And in the sweetest passage of a song.
Oh just beyond the fairest thoughts that throng
This breast, the thought of thee waits hidden
                                    yet bright;
But it must never, never come in sight;
I must stop short of thee the whole day long.
But when sleep comes to close each difficult day,
When night gives pause to the long watch I keep,
And all my bonds I needs must loose apart,
Must doff my will as raiment laid away –
   With the first dream that comes with the
                                    first sleep,
   I run, I run, I am gathered to thy heart.

ALICE MEYNELL

Love is Enough

Love is enough: though the world be a-waning,
And the woods have no voice but the voice of
           complaining,
Though the skies be too dark for dim eyes to
           discover
The gold-cups and daisies fair blooming
           thereunder,
Though the hills be held shadows, and the sea a
           dark wonder,
And this day draw a veil over all deeds passed
           over,
Yet their hands shall not tremble, their feet
           shall not falter:
The void shall not weary, the fear shall not alter
These lips and these eyes of the loved and
           the lover.

WILLIAM MORRIS

Elegy to his Mistress

Be just, dear Maid, an equal passion prove,
Or show me cause why I should ever love.
I do not at your cold disdain repine,
Nor ask your love, do you but suffer mine.
I dare not aim at more exalted bliss,
And Venus will bestow her votary this.
Take him who will for endless ages serve;
Take him, whose faithful flame will never
                                    swerve.
Though no illustrious names my race adorn,
Who am but of *Equestrian* order born;
Though a few ploughs serve my paternal
                                    fields,
Nor my small table many dishes yields;
Yet Bacchus, Phoebus, and the tuneful nine,
Are all my friends, and to my side incline,
And love's great god, at last, will make me
                                    thine.
Heaven knows, dear Maid, I love no other fair;
In thee lives all my love, my heaven lies there.
Oh! may I by indulgent fate's decree
With thee lead all my life, and die with thee.
Thy beauties yield me my transporting theme,
And while I celebrate thy charming name,
My verse shall be as sacred as my flame.
Jove's several rapes, his injur'd Io's wrongs,
Are made immortal in his poet's songs.

Verse still reveals whence Leda's flames began,
Rais'd by the secret godhead in the swan.
The story of the rape Europa bore,
Shall last while winds shall rage, or waters
roar.
Your name shall live like theirs, while verse
endures,
And mine be ever writ, and read with yours.

OVID

(translated by Charles Hopkins)

A Bunch of Roses

Roses ruddy and roses white,
  What are the joys that my heart discloses?
Sitting alone in the fading light
Memories come to me here tonight
  With the wonderful scent of the big red roses.

Memories come as the daylight fades
  Down on the hearth where the firelight dozes;
Flicker and flutter the lights and shades,
And I see the face of a queen of maids
  Whose memory comes with the scent of roses.

Visions arise of a scene of mirth,
  And a ballroom belle who superbly poses –
A queenly woman of queenly worth,
And I am the happiest man on earth
  With a single flower from a bunch of roses.

Only her memory lives tonight –
  God in His wisdom her young life closes;
Over her grave may the turf be light,
Cover her coffin with roses white
  She was always fond of the big white roses.

*   *   *

Such are the visions that fade away –
  Man proposes and God disposes;
Look in the glass and I see today
Only an old man, worn and grey,
  Bending his head to a bunch of roses.

'BANJO' PATERSON

Annabel Lee

It was many and many a year ago,
    In a kingdom by the sea,
That a maiden lived whom you may know
    By the name of Annabel Lee;
And this maiden she lived with no other thought
    Than to love and be loved by me.

I was a child and *she* was a child,
    In this kingdom by the sea,
But we loved with a love that was more than love –
    I and my Annabel Lee;
With a love that the wingèd seraphs of Heaven
    Coveted her and me.

And this was the reason that, long ago,
    In this kingdom by the sea,
A wind blew out of a cloud, chilling
    My beautiful Annabel Lee;
So that her high-born kinsman came
    And bore her away from me,
To shut her up in a sepulchre
    In this kingdom by the sea.

The angels, not half so happy in Heaven,
    Went envying her and me;
Yes! that was the reason (as all men know,
    In this kingdom by the sea)
That the wind came out of the cloud by night,
    Chilling and killing my Annabel Lee.

But our love it was stronger by far than the love
    Of those who were older than we –
    Of many far wiser than we –
And neither the angels in Heaven above,
    Nor the demons down under the sea,
Can ever dissever my soul from the soul
    Of the beautiful Annabel Lee:

For the moon never beams without bringing
                    me dreams
    Of the beautiful Annabel Lee;
And the stars never rise but I see the bright eyes
    Of the beautiful Annabel Lee;
And so, all the night-tide, I lie down by the side
Of my darling, my darling, my life and my bride,
    In her sepulchre there by the sea –
    In her tomb by the sounding sea.

EDGAR ALLAN POE

A Dream within a Dream

Take this kiss upon the brow!
And, in parting from you now,
Thus much let me avow –
You are not wrong, who deem
That my days have been a dream;
Yet if hope has flown away
In a night, or in a day,
In a vision, or in none,
Is it therefore the less *gone*?
All that we see or seem
Is but a dream within a dream.

I stand amid the roar
Of a surf-tormented shore,
And I hold within my hand
Grains of the golden sand –
How few! yet how they creep
Through my fingers to the deep,
While I weep – while I weep!
O God! can I not grasp
Them with a tighter clasp?
O God! can I not save
One from the pitiless wave?
Is *all* that we see or seem
But a dream within a dream?

EDGAR ALLAN POE

Echo

Come to me in the silence of the night:
   Come in the speaking silence of a dream;
Come with soft rounded cheeks and eyes as bright
   As sunlight on a stream;
     Come back in tears,
O memory, hope, love of finished years.

O dream how sweet, too sweet, too bitter sweet,
   Whose wakening should have been in Paradise,
Where souls brimful of love abide and meet;
   Where thirsting, longing eyes
     Watch the slow door
That opening, letting in, lets out no more.

Yet come to me in dreams, that I may live
   My very life again though cold in death:
Come back to me in dreams, that I may give
   Pulse for pulse, breath for breath:
     Speak low, lean low,
As long ago, my love, how long ago!

CHRISTINA ROSSETTI

Remember

Remember me when I am gone away,
Gone far away into the silent land;
When you can no more hold me by the hand,
Nor I half turn to go, yet turning stay.
Remember me when no more, day by day.
You tell me of our future that you planned;
Only remember me; you understand
It will be late to counsel then or pray.
Yet if you should forget me for a while
And afterwards remember, do not grieve;
For if the darkness and corruption leave
A vestige of the thoughts that once I had,
Better by far you should forget and smile
Than that you should remember and be sad.

CHRISTINA ROSSETTI

The First Day

I wish I could remember the first day,
First hour, first moment of your meeting me,
If bright or dim the season, it might be
Summer or Winter for aught I can say;
So unrecorded did it slip away,
So blind was I to see and to foresee,
So dull to mark the budding of my tree
That would not blossom yet for many a May.

If only I could recollect it, such
A day of days! I let it come and go
As traceless as a thaw of bygone snow;
It seemed to mean so little, meant so much;
If only now I could recall that touch,
First touch of hand in hand – Did one but know!

CHRISTINA ROSSETTI

Silent Noon

Your hands lie open in the long fresh grass,
 The finger-points look through like rosy blooms;
Your eyes smile peace. The pasture gleams and glooms
 'Neath billowing skies that scatter and amass.
All round our nest, far as the eye can pass,
 Are golden kingcup fields with silver edge
Where the cow-parsley skirts the hawthorn hedge.
 'Tis visible silence, still as the hour-glass.

Deep in the sun-searched growths the dragon-fiy
 Hangs like a blue thread loosened from the sky:
So this wing'd hour is dropt to us from above.
 Oh! clasp we to our hearts, for deathless dower,
This close-companioned inarticulate hour
 When twofold silence was the song of love.

DANILE GABRIEL ROSSETTI

A Sudden Light

I have been here before,
　　But when or how I cannot tell:
I know the grass beyond the door,
　　The sweet keen smell,
The sighing sound, the lights around the shore.

You have been mine before –
　　How long ago I may not know:
But just when at that swallow's soar
　　Your neck turned so,
Some veil did fall – I knew it all of yore.

Has this been thus before?
　　And shall not thus time's eddying flight
Still with our lives our love restore
　　In death's despite,
And day and night yield one delight once more?

DANILE GABRIEL ROSSETTI

Sonnet 18

Shall I compare thee to a summer's day?
Thou art more lovely and more temperate:
Rough winds do shake the darling buds of May,
And summer's lease hath all too short a date:
Sometime too hot the eye of heaven shines,
And often is his gold complexion dimm'd;
And every fair from fair sometime declines,
By chance or nature's changing course untrimm'd;
But thy eternal summer shall not fade,
Nor lose possession of that fair thou ow'st,
Nor shall death brag thou wander'st in his shade,
When in eternal lines to time thou grow'st;
   So long as men can breathe, or eyes can see,
   So long lives this, and this gives life to thee.

WILLIAM SHAKESPEARE

Sonnet 130

My mistress' eyes are nothing like the sun;
Coral is far more red than her lips red;
If snow be white, why then her breasts are dun;
If hairs be wires, black wires grow on her head.
I have seen roses damask'd, red and white,
But no such roses see I in her cheeks;
And in some perfumes is there more delight
Than in the breath that from my mistress reeks.
I love to hear her speak, yet well I know
That music hath a far more pleasing sound;
I grant I never saw a goddess go:
My mistress, when she walks, treads on the ground.
  And yet, by heaven, I think my love as rare
  As any she belied with false compare.

WILLIAM SHAKESPEARE

Love's Philosophy

The fountains mingle with the river,
   And the rivers with the ocean;
The winds of heaven mix for ever,
   With a sweet emotion;
Nothing in the world is single;
   All things by a law divine
In one spirit meet and mingle –
   Why not I with thine?

See! the mountains kiss high heaven,
   And the waves clasp one another;
No sister flower would be forgiven,
   If it disdained it's brother;
And the sunlight clasps the earth,
   And the moonbeams kiss the sea;
What is all this sweet work worth,
   If thou kiss not me?

PERCY BYSSHE SHELLEY

To –

Music, when soft voices die,
Vibrates in the memory –
Odours, when sweet violets sicken,
Live within the sense they quicken.
Rose leaves, when the rose is dead,
Are heaped for the beloved's bed;
And so thy thoughts, when thou art gone,
Love itself shall slumber on.

PERCY BYSSHE SHELLEY

Good-Night

Good-night? ah! no; the hour is ill
  Which severs those it should unite;
Let us remain together still,
  Then it will be good night.

How can I call the lone night good,
  Though thy sweet wishes wing its flight?
Be it not said, thought, understood –
  Then it will be – good night.

To hearts which near each other move
  From evening close to morning light,
The night is good; because, my love,
  They never say good-night.

PERCY BYSSHE SHELLEY

Dead Love

Oh, never weep for love that's dead,
Since love is seldom true
But changes his fashion from blue to red,
From brightest red to blue,
And love was born to an early death
And is so seldom true.

Then harbour no smile on your bonny face
To win the deepest sigh.
The fairest words on truest lips
Pass on and surely die,
And you will stand alone, my dear,
When wintry winds draw nigh.

Sweet, never weep for what cannot be,
For this God has not given.
If the merest dream of love were true,
Then, sweet, we should be in heaven –
And this is only earth, my dear,
Where true love is not given.

ELIZABETH SIDDAL

Love and Sleep

Lying asleep between the strokes of night
  I saw my love lean over my sad bed,
  Pale as the duskiest lily's leaf or head,
Smooth-skinned and dark, with bare throat
                       made to bite,
Too wan for blushing and too warm for white,
  But perfect-coloured without white or red.
And her lips opened amorously, and said –
I wist not what, saving one word – Delight.

And all her face was honey to my mouth,
  And all her body pasture to mine eyes;
    The long lithe arms and hotter hands than fire,
The quivering flanks, hair smelling of the south,
  The bright light feet, the splendid supple thighs
  And glittering eyelids of my soul's desire.

ALGERNON CHARLES SWINBURNE

Come into the Garden, Maud

Come into the garden, Maud,
  For the black bat, night, has flown,
Come into the garden, Maud,
  I am here at the gate alone;
And the woodbine spices are wafted abroad,
  And the musk of the rose is blown.

For a breeze of morning moves,
  And the planet of Love is on high,
Beginning to faint in the light that she loves
  On a bed of daffodil sky,
To faint in the light of the sun she loves,
  To faint in his light, and to die.

All night have the roses heard
  The flute, violin, bassoon;
All night has the casement jessamine stirr'd
  To the dancers dancing in tune;
Till silence fell with the waking bird,
  And a hush with the setting moon.

I said to the lily, 'There is but one
  With whom she has heart to be gay.
When will the dancers leave her alone?
  She is weary of dance and play.'
Now half to the setting moon are gone,
  And half to the rising day;
Low on the sand and loud on the stone
  The last wheel echoes away.

I said to the rose, 'The brief night goes
   In babble and revel and wine.
O young lord-lover, what sighs are those,
   For one that will never be thine?
But mine, but mine,' I sware to the rose,
   'For ever and ever, mine.'

And the soul of the rose went into my blood,
   As the music clash'd in the hall:
And long by the garden lake I stood,
   For I heard your rivulet fall
From the lake to the meadow and on to the wood,
   Our wood, that is dearer than all;

From the meadow your walks have left so sweet
   That whenever a March-wind sighs
He sets the jewel-print of your feet
   In violets blue as your eyes,
To the woody hollows in which we meet
   And the valleys of Paradise.

The slender acacia would not shake
   One long milk-bloom on the tree;
The white lake-blossom fell into the lake
   As the pimpernel dozed on the lea;
But the rose was awake all night for your sake,
   Knowing your promise to me;
The lilies and roses were all awake,
   They sigh'd for the dawn and thee.

   Queen rose of the rosebud garden of girls,
     Come hither, the dances are done,

In gloss of satin and glimmer of pearls,
    Queen lily and rose in one;
Shine out, little head, sunning over with curls,
    To the flowers, and be their sun.

There has fallen a splendid tear
    From the passion-flower at the gate.
She is coming, my dove, my dear;
    She is coming, my life, my fate;
The red rose cries, 'She is near, she is near;'
    And the white rose weeps, 'She is late;'
The larkspur listens, 'I hear, I hear;'
    And the lily whispers, 'I wait.'

She is coming, my own, my sweet;
    Were it ever so airy a tread,
My heart would hear her and beat,
    Were it earth in an earthy bed;
My dust would hear her and beat,
    Had I lain for a century dead;
Would start and tremble under her feet,
    And blossom in purple and red.

ALFRED LORD TENNYSON

from *Maud,* Part 1, XXII

Oh That 'twere Possible

Oh that 'twere possible
   After long grief and pain
To find the arms of my true love
   Round me once again!

When I was wont to meet her
   In the silent woody places
Of the land that gave me birth,
   We stood tranced in long embraces
Mixed with kisses sweeter, sweeter,
   Than anything on earth.

A shadow flits before me,
   Not thou, but like to thee;
Ah Christ, that it were possible
   For one short hour to see
The souls we loved, that they might tell us
   What and where they be.

It leads me forth at evening,
   It lightly winds and steals
In a cold white robe before me,
   When all my spirit reels
At the shouts, the leagues of lights,
   And the roaring of the wheels.

Half the night I waste in sighs,
   Half in dreams I sorrow after

The delight of early skies;
   In a wakeful doze I sorrow
For the hand, the lips, the eyes,
   For the meeting of the morrow,
The delight of happy laughter,
   The delight of low replies.

ALFRED LORD TENNYSON

Now *S*leeps the Crimson Petal

Now sleeps the crimson petal, now the white;
Nor waves the cypress in the palace walk;
Nor winks the gold fin in the porphyry font:
The firefly wakens: waken thou with me.

Now droops the milk-white peacock like a ghost,
And like a ghost she glimmers on to me.

Now lies the earth all Danaë to the stars,
And all thy heart lies open unto me.

Now slides the silent meteor on, and leaves
A shining furrow, as thy thoughts in me.

Now folds the lily all her sweetness up,
And slips into the bosom of the lake:
So fold thyself, my dearest, thou, and slip
Into my bosom and be lost in me.

ALFRED LORD TENNYSON

No One So Much As You

No one so much as you
Loves this my clay,
Or would lament as you
Its dying day.

You know me through and through
Though I have not told,
And though with what you know
You are not bold.

None ever was so fair
As I thought you;
Not a word can I bear
Spoken against you.

All that I ever did
For you seemed coarse
Compared with what I hid
Nor put in force.

My eyes scarce dare meet you
Lest they should prove
I but respond to you
And do not love.

We look and understand,
We cannot speak –
Except in trifles and
Words the most weak.

For I at most accept
Your love, regretting
That is all: I have kept
Only a fretting

That I could not return
All that you gave
And could not ever burn
With the love you have,

Till sometimes it did seem
Better it were
Never to see you more
Than linger here

With only gratitude
Instead of love –
A pine in solitude
Cradling a dove.

EDWARD THOMAS

This is the Female Form

This is the female form,
A divine nimbus exhales from it from head to foot,
It attracts with fierce undeniable attraction,
I am drawn by its breath as if I were no more
    than a helpless vapor, all falls aside but
    myself and it,
Books, art, religion, time, the visible and solid
    earth, and what was expected of heaven or
    fear'd of hell, are now consumed,
Mad filaments, ungovernable shoots play out of
    it, the response likewise ungovernable,
Hair, bosom, hips, bend of legs, negligent falling
    hands all diffused, mine too diffused,
Ebb stung by the flow and flow stung by the ebb,
    love-flesh swelling and deliciously aching,
Limitless limpid jets of love hot and enormous,
    quivering jelly of love, white-blow and
    delirious juice,
Bridegroom night of love working surely and
    softly into the prostrate dawn,
Undulating into the willing and yielding day,
Lost in the cleave of the clasping and sweet-
    flesh'd day.

WALT WHITMAN

from *I Sing the Body Electric*, Stanza 5

Friendship after Love

After the fierce midsummer all ablaze
   Has burned itself to ashes, and expires
   In the intensity of its own fires,
There come the mellow, mild, St Martin days,
Crowned with the calm of peace, but sad with haze.
   So after love has led us, till he tires
   Of his own throes, and torments, and desires,
Comes large-eyed friendship: with a restful gaze,
He beckons us to follow, and across
   Cool verdant vales we wander free from care.
   Is it a touch of frost lies in the air?
Why are we haunted with a sense of loss?
We do not wish the pain back, or the heat;
And yet, and yet, these days are incomplete.

ELLA WHEELER WILCOX

Hélas!

To drift with every passion till my soul
Is a stringed lute on which all winds can play,
Is it for this that I have given away
Mine ancient wisdom, and austere control?
Methinks my life is a twice-written scroll
Scrawled over on some boyish holiday
With idle songs for pipe and virelay,
Which do but mar the secret of the whole.
Surely there was a time I might have trod
The sunlit heights, and from life's dissonance
Struck one clear chord to reach the ears of God.
Is that time dead? lo! with a little rod
I did but touch the honey of romance –
And must I lose a soul's inheritance?

OSCAR WILDE

We are Made One with What We Touch and See

We are resolved into the supreme air,
   We are made one with what we touch and see,
With our heart's blood each crimson sun is fair,
   With our young lives each spring-
                     impassioned tree
Flames into green, the wildest beasts that range
The moor our kinsmen are, all life is one, and
                     all is change.

With beat of systole and of diastole
   One grand great life throbs through earth's
                     giant heart,
And mighty waves of single Being roll
   From nerveless germ to man, for we are part
Of every rock and bird and beast and hill,
One with the things that prey on us, and one
                     with what we kill . . .

One sacrament are consecrate, the earth
   Not we alone hath passions hymeneal,
The yellow buttercups that shake for mirth
   At daybreak know a pleasure not less real
Than we do, when in some fresh-blossoming wood
We draw the spring into our hearts, and feel
                     that life is good . . .

Is the light vanished from our golden sun,
   Or is this daedal-fashioned earth less fair,
That we are nature's heritors, and one
   With every pulse of life that beats the air?
Rather new suns across the sky shall pass,
New splendour come unto the flower, new
                        glory to the grass.

And we two lovers shall not sit afar,
   Critics of nature, but the joyous sea
Shall be our raiment, and the bearded star
   Shoot arrows at our pleasure! We shall be
Part of the mighty universal whole,
And through all aeons mix and mingle with
                        the kosmic soul!

We shall be notes in that great symphony
   Whose cadence circles through the
                        rhythmic spheres,
And all the live world's throbbing heart shall be
   One with our heart, the stealthy creeping years
Have lost their terrors now, we shall not die,
The universe itself shall be our immortality!

OSCAR WILDE

from *Panthea*

A Drinking Song

Wine comes in at the mouth
And love comes in at the eye;
That's all we shall know for truth
Before we grow old and die.
I lift the glass to my mouth,
I look at you, and I sigh.

W. B. YEATS

The Ragged Wood

O hurry where by water among the trees
The delicate-stepping stag and his lady sigh,
When they have but looked upon their images –
Would none had ever loved but you and I!

Or have you heard that sliding silver-shoed
Pale silver-proud queen-woman of the sky,
When the sun looked out of his golden hood? –
O that none ever loved but you and I!

O hurry to the ragged wood, for there
I will drive all those lovers out and cry –
O my share of the world, O yellow hair!
No one has ever loved but you and I!

W. B. YEATS

A Poet to His Beloved

I bring you with reverent hands
The books of my numberless dreams,
White woman that passion has worn
As the tide wears the dove-grey sands,
And with heart more old than the horn
That is brimmed from the pale fire of time:
White woman with numberless dreams,
I bring you my passionate rhyme.

W. B. YEATS

Famous
Love
Letters

Ludwig van Beethoven to a lady unknown

6th July, in the morning

My angel, my everything, my very self – only a few words today, and in pencil (with yours) – I shall not be certain of my rooms here until tomorrow – what an unnecessary waste of time – why this deep grief, where necessity speaks – can our love exist but by sacrifices, by not demanding everything. Can you change it, that you are not completely mine, that I am not completely yours? Oh God, look upon beautiful Nature and calm your mind about what must be – love demands everything and completely with good reason, that is how it is <u>for me with you, and for you with me</u> – only you forget too easily that I must live <u>for myself and for you as well</u>; if we were wholly united, you would not feel this as painfully, just as little as I would. My journey was terrible. I did not arrive here until 4 o'clock yesterday morning. As there were few horses, the mail coach chose another route, but what a dreadful one this was! At the last stage but one I was warned not to travel at night; attempts were made to frighten me about a forest, but that only made me more eager. I was wrong. The coach broke down on the awful road, a road without a proper surface, a country one. If the two coachmen had not been with me, I would have remained stranded on the way. Esterhazi travelled the usual road here and had the same fate with eight horses that I had with four. Yet I did get some pleasure out of it, as I always do when I successfully overcome difficulties. Now quickly to the interior from the exterior. We will probably see each other soon, only today I cannot convey to you my observations which I made during these few days about my life. If our hearts were always close together, I would have no such thoughts. My heart is full with so much to tell you. Oh, there are moments when I feel that language is nothing at all! Cheer up – remain my faithful only darling, my everything, as I for you, the rest is up to the gods, what must be for us and what is in store for us.

Your faithful Ludwig

Monday evening, 6th July
You are suffering, you my dearest creature – only now do I realise that letters have to be posted very early, on Mondays or Thursdays – the only days when the mail is delivered to K. – You are suffering – Oh, wherever I am, you are with me, I talk to myself and to you, arrange it that I can live with you; what a life!!!! as it is!!!! without you – Pursued by the goodness of mankind here and there, the goodness that I wish to deserve as little as I deserve it. Man's humility towards man – this pains me – and when I consider myself in relation to the universe, what am I and what is the man who is called the greatest? – And yet, therein lies the divine element in man. I weep when I think that you will probably not receive

first news of me until Saturday. However, as much as you love me – I love you even more deeply, but – but never hide yourself from me. Good-night – as I am taking the baths I must go to bed. Oh, go with me, go with me. Oh God – so near! so far! Is not our love a true edifice in Heaven – but also as firm as the firmament?

Good-morning, on 7th July.

While still in bed my thoughts turn towards you my Immortal Beloved, now and then happy, then sad again, waiting whether fate might answer us – I can only live either wholly with you or not at all; yes, I have resolved to stray about in the distance, until I can fly into your arms, and send my soul embraced by you into the realm of the Spirits – yes, unfortunately it must be – you will compose yourself all the more since you know my faithfulness to you, never can another own my heart, never – never. O God, why do I have to separate from someone whom I love so much, and yet my life in Vienna as it is now is a miserable life – your love makes me at once most happy and most unhappy – at my age I would now need some conformity, some regularity of my life – can this exist in our relationship? – Angel, I have just heard that the mail coach goes every day – and thus I must finish so that you may receive the letter immediately. Be patient – only through quiet contemplation of our existence can we achieve our purpose to live together. Be calm; for only by calmly considering our lives can we achieve our purpose of living together. Be calm – love me – today – yesterday – What yearning with tears for you – you – you, my life – my everything – farewell – oh, continue to love me – never misjudge the most faithful heart of your Beloved

L

Ever Thine
Ever Mine
Ever Ours.

Napoleon Bonaparte to Josephine Bonaparte

Nice, 10 Germinal, year IV [1796]

I have not spent a day without loving you; I have not spent a night without embracing you; I have not so much as drunk a single cup of tea without cursing the pride and ambition which force me to remain separated from the moving spirit of my life. In the midst of my duties, whether I am at the head of my army or inspecting the camps, my beloved Josephine stands alone in my heart, occupies my mind, fills my thoughts.

If I am moving away from you with the speed of the Rhône torrent, it is only that I may see you again more quickly. If I rise to work in the middle of the night, it is because this may hasten by a matter of days the arrival of my sweet love. Yet in your letters of the 23rd and 26th Ventôse, you call me *vous*. *Vous* yourself! Ah! wretch, how could you have written this letter? How cold it is? And then there are those four days between the 23rd and the 26th; what were you doing that you failed to write to your husband? . . . Ah, my love, that *vous*, those four days made me long for my former indifference. Woe to the person responsible! May he as punishment and penalty experience what my convictions and the evidence (which is in your friend's favour) would make me experience! Hell has no torments great enough! Nor do the Furies have serpents enough! *Vous*! *Vous*! Ah! how will things stand in two weeks? . . . My spirit is heavy; my heart is fettered and I am terrified by my fantasies . . . You love me less; but you will get over the loss. One day you will love me no longer; at least tell me; then I shall know how I have come to deserve this misfortune . . . Farewell, my wife: the torment, joy, hope and moving spirit of my life; whom I love, whom I fear, who fills me with tender feelings which draw me close to Nature, and with violent impulses as tumultuous as thunder. I ask of you neither eternal love, nor fidelity, but simply . . . *truth*, unlimited honesty. The day when you say 'I love you less' will mark the end of my love and the last day of my life. If my heart were base enough to love without being loved in return I would tear it to pieces. Josephine! Josephine! Remember what I have sometimes said to you: Nature has endowed me with a virile and decisive character. It has built yours out of lace and gossamer. Have you ceased to love me? Forgive me, love of my life, my soul is racked by conflicting forces.

My heart, obsessed by you, is full of fears which prostrate me with misery . . . I am distressed not to be calling you by name. I shall wait for you to write it.

Farewell! Ah! if you love me less you can never have loved me. In that case I shall truly be pitiable.

Bonaparte

P.S. The war this year has changed beyond recognition. I have had meat, bread and fodder distributed; my armed cavalry will soon be on the march. My soldiers are showing inexpressible confidence in me; you alone are a source of chagrin to me; you alone are the joy and torment of my life. I send a kiss to your children, whom you do not mention. By God! If you did, your letters would be half as long again. Then visitors at ten o'clock in the morning would not have the pleasure of seeing you. Woman!!!

Lewis Carroll to Gertrude

Christ Church, Oxford, 28th October 1876

My dearest Gertrude – You will be sorry, and surprised, and puzzled, to hear what a queer illness I have had ever since you went. I sent for the doctor, and said, 'Give me some medicine, for I'm tired.' He said, 'Nonsense and stuff! You don't want medicine: go to bed!' I said, 'No; it isn't the sort of tiredness that wants bed. I'm tired in the *face*.' He looked a little grave, and said, 'Oh, it's your *nose* that's tired: a person often talks too much when he thinks he nose a great deal.' I said, 'No, it isn't the nose. Perhaps it's the *hair*.' Then he looked rather grave, and said, '*Now* I understand: you've been playing too many hairs on the pianoforte.' 'No, indeed I haven't!' I said, 'and it isn't exactly the *hair*: it's more about the nose and chin.' Then he looked a good deal graver, and said, 'Have you been walking much on your chin lately?' I said, 'No.' 'Well!' he said, 'it puzzles me very much. Do you think it's in the lips?' 'Of course!' I said. 'That's exactly what it is!'

Then he looked very grave indeed, and said, 'I think you must have been giving too many kisses.' 'Well,' I said, 'I did give one kiss to a baby child, a little friend of mine.' 'Think again,' he said; 'are you sure it was only one?' I thought again, and said, 'Perhaps it was eleven times.' Then the doctor said, 'You must not give her any more till

120

your lips are quite rested again.' 'But what am I to do?' I said, 'because you see, I owe her a hundred and eighty-two more.' Then he looked so grave that tears ran down his cheeks, and he said, 'You may send them to her in a box.'

Then I remembered a little box that I once bought at Dover, and thought I would someday give it to *some* little girl or other. So I have packed them all in it very carefully. Tell me if they come safe or if any are lost on the way.

Lewis Carroll

Honoré de Balzac to Evelina Hanska

Sunday, 19th June 1836

My beloved angel – I am nearly mad about you, as much as one can be mad: I cannot bring together two ideas that you do not interpose yourself between.

I can no longer think of anything but you. In spite of myself, my imagination carries me to you. I grasp you, I kiss you, I caress you, a thousand of the most amorous caresses take possession of me.

As for my heart, there you will always be – very much so. I have a delicious sense of you there. But, my God, what is to become of me if you have deprived me of my reason? This is a monomania which, this morning, terrifies me.

I rise up every moment saying to myself, 'Come, I am going there!' Then I sit down again, moved by the sense of my obligations. There is a frightful conflict. This is not life. I have never before been like that. You have devoured everything.

I feel foolish and happy as soon as I think of you. I whirl round in a delicious dream in which in one instant I live a thousand years. What a horrible situation!

Overcome with love, feeling love in every pore, living only for love, and seeing oneself consumed by griefs and caught in a thousand spiders' threads.

Oh, my darling Eva, you did not know it. I picked up your card. It is there before me, and I talk to you as if you were there. I see you, as I did yesterday, beautiful, astonishingly beautiful.

Yesterday, during the whole evening, I said to myself, 'She is mine!' Ah! The angels are not as happy in Paradise as I was yesterday!

Gustave Flaubert to Louise Colet

15th August 1846

I will cover you with love when next I see you, with caresses, with ecstasy. I want to gorge you with all the joys of the flesh, so that you faint and die. I want you to be amazed by me, and to confess to yourself that you had never even dreamed of such transports . . . When you are old, I want you to recall those few hours, I want your dry bones to quiver with joy when you think of them.

Victor Hugo to Adele Foucher

My dearest – When two souls, which have sought each other for however long in the throng, have finally found each other . . . a union, fiery and pure as they themselves are . . . begins on earth and continues for ever in heaven.

This union is love, true love . . . a religion which deifies the loved one, whose life comes from devotion and passion, and for which the greatest sacrifices are the sweetest delights.

This is the love which you inspire in me . . . Your soul is made to love with the purity and passion of angels; but perhaps it can only love another angel, in which case I must tremble with apprehension.

Yours for ever,
Victor Hugo

James Joyce to Nora Barnacle

15th August 1904

My dear Nora – It has just struck me. I came in at half past eleven. Since then I have been sitting in an easy chair like a fool. I could do nothing. I hear nothing but your voice. I am like a fool hearing you call me 'Dear'. I offended two men today by leaving them coolly. I wanted to hear your voice, not theirs.

When I am with you I leave aside my contemptuous, suspicious nature. I wish I felt your head on my shoulder. I think I will go to bed.

I have been a half-hour writing this thing. Will you write something to me? I hope you will. How am I to sign myself? I won't sign anything at all, because I don't know what to sign myself.

Franz Kafka to Felice Bauer

11th November 1912

Fräulein Felice!

I am now going to ask you a favour which sounds quite crazy, and which I should regard as such were I the one to receive the letter. It is also the very greatest test that even the kindest person could be put to. Well, this is it:

Write to me only once a week, so that your letter arrives on Sunday – for I cannot endure your daily letters, I am incapable of enduring them. For instance, I answer one of your letters, then lie in bed in apparent calm, but my heart beats through my entire body and is conscious only of you. I belong to you; there is really no other way of expressing it, and that is not strong enough. But for this very reason I don't want to know what you are wearing; it confuses me so much that I cannot deal with life; and that's why I don't want to know that you are fond of me. If I did, how could I, fool that I am, go on sitting in my office, or here at home, instead of leaping on to a train with my eyes shut and opening them only when I am with you? Oh, there is a sad, sad reason for not doing so. To make it short: My health is only just good enough for myself alone, not good enough for marriage, let alone fatherhood. Yet when I read your letter, I feel I could overlook even what cannot possibly be overlooked.

If only I had your answer now! And how horribly

I torment you, and how I compel you, in the stillness of your room, to read this letter, as nasty a letter as has ever lain on your desk! Honestly, it strikes me sometimes that I prey like a spectre on your felicitous name! If only I had mailed Saturday's letter, in which I implored you never to write to me again, and in which I gave a similar promise. Oh God, what prevented me from sending that letter? All would be well. But is a peaceful solution possible now? Would it help if we wrote to each other only once a week? No, if my suffering could be cured by such means it would not be serious. And already I foresee that I shan't be able to endure even the Sunday letters. And so, to compensate for Saturday's lost opportunity, I ask you with what energy remains to me at the end of this letter: If we value our lives, let us abandon it all.

Did I think of signing myself *Dein*? No, nothing could be more false. No, I am for ever fettered to myself, that's what I am, and that's what I must try to live with.

Franz

King Henry VIII to Anne Boleyn

[*c.1528*]

In debating with myself the contents of your letters I have been put to a great agony; not knowing how to understand them, whether to my disadvantage as shown in some places, or to my advantage as in others. I beseech you now with all my heart definitely to let me know your whole mind as to the love between us; for necessity compels me to plague you to reply, having been for more than a year now struck by the dart of love, and being uncertain either of failure or of finding a place in your heart and affection, which point has certainly kept me for some time from naming you my mistress, since if you only love me with an ordinary love the name is not appropriate to you, seeing that it stands for an uncommon position very remote from the ordinary; but if it pleases you to do the duty of a true, loyal mistress and friend, and to give yourself body and heart to me, who have been, and will be, your very loyal servant (if your rigour does not forbid me), I promise you that not only the name will be due to you, but also to take you as my sole mistress, casting off all others than yourself out of mind and affection, and to serve you only; begging you to make me a complete reply to this rude letter as to how far and in what I can trust; and if it does not please you to reply in writing, to let me know of some place where I can have it by word of mouth, the which place I will seek out with all my heart. No more, for fear of wearying you. Written by the hand of him who would winningly remain your

HR

Michael Faraday to Sarah Barnard

Royal Institution

Thursday evening [*December 1820*]

My dear Sarah – It is astonishing how much the state of the body influences the powers of the mind. I have been thinking all the morning of the very delightful and interesting letter I would send you this evening, and now I am so tired, and yet have so much to do, that my thoughts are quite giddy and run round your image without any power of themselves to stop and admire it. I want to say a thousand kind and, believe me, heartfelt things to you, but am not master of words fit for the purpose; and still, as I ponder and think on you, chlorides, trials, oil, Davy, steel, miscellanea, mercury and fifty other professional fancies swim before and drive me further and further into the quandary of stupidity.

From your affectionate

Michael

Zelda Sayre to F. Scott Fitzgerald

Spring 1919

Sweetheart – Please, please don't be so depressed. We'll be married soon, and then these lonesome nights will be over for ever – and until we are, I am loving, loving every tiny minute of the day and night.

Maybe you won't understand this, but sometimes when I miss you most, it's hardest to write – and you always know when I make myself. Just the ache of it all – and I can't tell you.

If we were together, you'd feel how strong it is – you're so sweet when you're melancholy. I love your sad tenderness when I've hurt you. That's one of the reasons I could never be sorry for our quarrels – and they bothered you so. Those dear, dear little fusses, when I always tried so hard to make you kiss and forget.

Scott – there's nothing in all the world I want but you – and your precious love. All the material things are nothing. I'd just hate to live a sordid, colourless existence, because you'd soon love me less – and less – and I'd do anything – anything – to keep your heart for my own. I don't want to live – I want to love first, and live incidentally . . .

Don't – don't ever think of the things you can't give me. You've trusted me with the dearest heart of all – and it's so damn much more than anybody else in all the world has ever had –

How can you think deliberately of life without me? If you should die – Oh darling, darling Scott – it'd be like going blind . . . I'd have no purpose in life – be just a pretty decoration.

Don't you think I was made for you? I feel like you had me ordered and I was delivered to you – to be worn – I want you to wear me, like a watch-charm or a button-hole bouquet – to the world.

And then, when we're alone, I want to help – to know that you can't do anything without me . . .

All my heart –

I love you

Zelda Fitzgerald to F. Scott Fitzgerald

[*1920*]

I look down the tracks and see you coming – and out of every haze & mist your darling rumpled trousers are hurrying to me – Without you, dearest dearest, I couldn't see or hear or feel or think – or live – I love you so and I'm never in all our lives going to let us be apart another night. It's like begging for mercy of a storm or killing Beauty or growing old, without you. I want to kiss you so – and in the back where your dear hair starts and your chest – I love you – and I can't tell you how much – To think that I'll *die* without your knowing – Goofo, you've *got* to try [to] feel how much I do – how inanimate I am when you're gone – I can't even hate these damnable people – Nobody's got any right to live but us – and they're dirtying up our world and I can't hate them because I want you so – Come Quick – Come Quick to me – I could never do without you if you hated me and were covered with sores like a leper – if you ran away with another woman and starved me and beat me – I still would want you I *know* –

Lover, Lover, Darling –

Your Wife

Oscar Wilde to Lord Alfred Douglas

January 1893, Babbacombe Cliff

My own boy – Your sonnet is quite lovely, and it is a marvel that those red rose-leaf lips of yours should be made no less for the madness of music and song than for the madness of kissing. Your slim gilt soul walks between passion and poetry. I know Hyacinthus, whom Apollo loved so madly, was you in Greek days. Why are you alone in London, and when do you go to Salisbury? Do go there to cool your hands in the grey twilight of Gothic things, and come here whenever you like. It is a lovely place and lacks only you; but go to Salisbury first.

Always, with undying love,

Yours, Oscar

March 1893, Savoy Hotel

Dearest of all boys – Your letter was delightful, red and yellow wine to me; but I am sad and out of sorts. Bosie, you must not make scenes with me. They kill me, they wreck the loveliness of life. I cannot see you, so Greek and gracious, distorted with passion. I cannot listen to your curved lips saying hideous things to me. I would sooner be blackmailed by every renter in London than to have you bitter, unjust, hating. You are the divine thing I want, the thing of grace and beauty; but I don't know how to do it. Shall I come to Salisbury?

My bill here is 49 pounds for a week. I have also got a new sitting-room over the Thames. Why are you not here, my dear, my wonderful boy? I fear I must leave; no money, no credit, and a heart of lead.

Your own, Oscar

Rouen, August 1897

My own darling boy – I got your telegram half an hour ago, and just send a line to say that I feel that my only hope of again doing beautiful work in art is being with you. It was not so in the old days, but now it is different, and you can really recreate in me that energy and sense of joyous power on which art depends. Everyone is furious with me for going back to you, but they don't understand us. I feel that it is only with you that I can do anything at all. Do remake my ruined life for me, and then our friendship and love will have a different meaning to the world. I wish that when we met at Rouen we had not parted at all. There are such wide abysses now of space and land between us. But we love each other.

Good-night, dear.

Ever yours, Oscar

(see also pages 151–5)

Lord Byron to Lady Caroline Lamb

August 1812

My dearest Caroline – If tears, which you saw & know I am not apt to shed, if the agitation in which I parted from you – agitation which you must have perceived through the *whole* of this most *nervous* affair – did not commence till the moment of leaving you approached, if all that I have said & done, & am still but too ready to say & do, have not sufficiently proved what my real feelings are & must be ever towards you, my love, I have no other proof to offer.

God knows I wish you happy, & when I quit you, or rather when you from a sense of duty to your husband & mother quit me, you shall acknowledge the truth of what I again promise & vow, that no other in word or deed shall ever hold the place in my affection which is & shall be most sacred to you till I am nothing.

I never knew till *that moment*, the *madness* of – my dearest & most beloved friend, I cannot express myself – this is no time for words – but I shall have a pride, a melancholy pleasure, in suffering what you yourself can hardly conceive, for you do not know me. I am now about to go out with a heavy heart, because my appearing this evening will stop any absurd story which the events of today might give rise to. Do you think *now* that I am *cold* & *stern* & *artful*? Will even *others* think so? Will your *mother* even – that mother to whom we must indeed sacrifice much, much more on my part than she shall ever know or can imagine?

'Promise not to love you!' ah, Caroline it is past promising. But I shall attribute all concessions to the proper motive & never cease to feel all that you have already witnessed & more than can ever be known but to my own heart – perhaps to yours. May God protect, forgive & bless you. Ever & even more than ever,

Your most attached

Byron

PS These taunts have driven you to this, my dearest Caroline; were it not for your mother and the kindness of your connections, is there anything on earth or heaven that would have made me so happy as to have made you mine long ago? and not less *now* than *then*, but *more* than ever at this time. You know I would with pleasure give up all here and all beyond the grave for you, and, in refraining from this, must my motives be misunderstood? I care not who knows this, what use is made of it – it is to *you* and to *you* only that they are *yourself*. I was and am yours freely and most entirely to obey, to honour, love – and fly with you when, where, and how you yourself *might* and *may* determine.

Robert Burns

Dear Madam – The passion of love has need to be productive of much delight, as where it takes thorough possession of the man it almost unfits him for anything else. The lover who is certain of an equal return of affection is surely the happiest of men; but he who is a prey to the horrors of anxiety and dreaded disappointment is a being whose situation is by no means enviable.

Of this, my present experience gives me much proof. To me, amusement seems impertinent, and business intrusion, while you alone engross every faculty of my mind.

May I request you to drop me a line to inform me when I may wait upon you? For pity's sake, do; and let me have it soon.

In the meantime allow me, in all the artless sincerity of truth, to assure you that I truly am, my dearest madam,

Your ardent lover, and devoted humble servant.

Jack London to Anna Strunsky

Dear Anna – Did I say that the humans might be filed in categories? Well, and if I did, let me qualify – not all humans. You elude me. I cannot place you, cannot grasp you. I may boast that of nine out of ten, under given circumstances, I can forecast their action; that of nine out of ten, by their word or action, I may feel the pulse of their hearts. But of the tenth I despair. It is beyond me. You are that tenth.

Were ever two souls, with dumb lips, more incongruously matched! We may feel in common – surely, we oftimes do – and when we do not feel in common, yet do we understand; and yet we have no common tongue. Spoken words do not come to us. We are unintelligible. God must laugh at the mummery.

The one gleam of sanity through it all is that we are both large temperamentally, large enough to often understand. True, we often understand but in vague glimmering ways, by dim perceptions, like ghosts, which, while we doubt, haunt us with their truth. And still, I, for one, dare not believe; for you are that tenth which I may not forecast.

Am I unintelligible now? I do not know. I imagine so. I cannot find the common tongue. Large temperamentally – that is it. It is the one thing that brings us at all in touch. We have flashed through us, you and I, each a bit of universal, and so we draw together. And yet we are so different.

I smile at you when you grow enthusiastic? It is a forgivable smile – nay, almost an envious smile. I have lived twenty-five years of repression. I learned not to be enthusiastic. It is a hard lesson to forget. I begin to forget, but it is so little. At the best, before I die, I cannot hope to forget all or most. I can exult, now that I am learning, in little things, in other things; but of my things, and secret things doubly mine, I cannot, I cannot. Do I make myself intelligible? Do you hear my voice? I fear not. There are poseurs. I am the most successful of them all.

Jack

John Keats to Fanny Brawne

March 1820

Sweetest Fanny – You fear, sometimes, I do not love you so much as you wish? My dear girl I love you ever and ever and without reserve. The more I have known you the more have I lov'd. In every way – even my jealousies have been agonies of love; in the hottest fit I ever had I would have died for you.

I have vex'd you too much. But for Love! Can I help it? You are always new. The last of your kisses was ever the sweetest; the last smile the brightest; the last movement the gracefullest. When you pass'd my window yesterday, I was fill'd with as much admiration as if I had then seen you for the first time.

You uttered a half- complaint once that I only lov'd your beauty. Have I nothing else then to love in you but that? Do not I see a heart naturally furnish'd with wings imprison itself with me? No ill prospect has been able to turn your thoughts a moment from me. This perhaps should be as much a subject of sorrow as joy – but I will not talk of that.

Even if you did not love me I could not help an entire devotion to you: how much more deeply then must I feel for you knowing you love me?

My mind has been the most discontented and restless one that ever was put into a body too small for it. I never felt my mind repose upon anything with complete and undistracted enjoyment – upon no person but you. When you are in the room my thoughts never fly out of the window: you always concentrate my whole senses.

The anxiety shown about our love in your last note is an immense pleasure to me; however you must not suffer such speculations to molest you any more; not will I any more believe you can have the least pique against me.

Brown is gone out – but here is Mrs Wylie – when she is gone I shall be awake for you.

Remembrances to your mother.

Your affectionate,

J. Keats

Oliver Cromwell to his wife Elizabeth

The Cockpit

My dearest – I have not leisure to write much, but I could chide thee that in many of thy letters thou writest to me that I should not be unmindful of thee and thy little ones. Truly, if I love thee not too well, I think I err not on the other hand much. Thou art dearer to me than any creature; let that suffice.

The Lord hath showed us an exceeding mercy: who can tell how great it is. My weak faith hath been upheld. I have been in my inward man marvellously supported, though, I assure thee, I grow an old man and feel infirmities of age marvellously stealing upon me. Would my corruptions did as fast decrease. Pray on my behalf in the latter respect.

The particulars of our late success Harry Vane or Gil Pickering will impart to thee.

My love to all dear friends.

I rest thine,

Oliver Cromwell

Jane Clairmont to Lord Byron

[*1815*]

You bid me write short to you and I have much to say. You also bade me believe that it was a fancy which made me cherish an attachment for you. It cannot be a fancy since you have been for the last year the object upon which every solitary moment led me to muse.

I do not expect you to love me, I am not worthy of your love. I feel you are superior, yet much to my surprise, more to my happiness, you betrayed passions I had believed no longer alive in your bosom.

Shall I also have to ruefully experience the want of happiness? Shall I reject it when it is offered? I may appear to you imprudent, vicious; my opinions detestable, my theory depraved; but one thing, at least, time shall show you: that I love gently and with affection, that I am incapable of anything approaching to the feeling of revenge or malice; I do assure you, your future will shall be mine, and everything you shall do or say, I shall not question.

Oscar Wilde to his Wife Constance

The Balmoral, Edinburgh
Tuesday, 16th December 1884

Dear and Beloved – Here am I, and you at the Antipodes. O execrable facts, that keep our lips from kissing, though our souls are one.

What can I tell you by letter? Alas! nothing that I would tell you. The messages of the gods to each other travel not by pen and ink and indeed your bodily presence here would not make you more real: for I feel your fingers in my hair, and your cheek brushing mine. The air is full of the music of your voice, my soul and body seem no longer mine, but mingled in some exquisite ecstasy with yours. I feel incomplete without you.

Ever and ever yours,

Oscar

Here I stay till Sunday.

A
Famous
Letter
from
Fiction

Oliver Mellors to Connie, Lady Chatterley

The Grange Farm, Old Heanor, 29 September
I got on here with a bit of contriving, because I knew Richards, the company engineer, in the army. It is a farm belonging to the Butler and Smitham Colliery Company, they use it for raising hay and oats for the pit-ponies; not a private concern. But they've got cows and pigs and all the rest of it, and I get thirty shillings a week as labourer. Rowley, the farmer, puts me on to as many jobs as he can, so that I can learn as much as possible between now and next Easter. I've not heard a thing about Bertha. I've no idea why she didn't show up at the divorce, nor where she is nor what she's up to. But if I keep quiet till March I suppose I shall be free. And don't you bother about Sir Clifford. He'll want to get rid of you one of these days. If he leaves you alone, it's a lot.

[. . .]

Never mind about Sir Clifford. If you don't hear anything from him, never mind. He can't really do anything to you. Wait, he will want to get rid of you at last, to cast you out. And if he doesn't, we'll manage to keep clear of him. But he will. In the end he will want to spew you out as the abominable thing.

Now I can't even leave off writing to you.

But a great deal of us is together, and we can but abide by it, and steer our courses to meet soon. John Thomas says good-night to Lady Jane, a little droopingly, but with a hopeful heart.

from *Lady Chatterley's Lover*, D. H. LAWRENCE

A
Lover's
Reproach

Oscar Wilde to Lord Alfred Douglas

H. M. Prison, Reading [*January–March 1897*]
Dear Bosie – After long and fruitless waiting I
have determined to write to you myself, as much
for your sake as for mine, as I would not like to
think that I had passed through two long years of
imprisonment without ever having received a
single line from you, or any news or message
even, except such as gave me pain.

Our ill-fated and most lamentable friendship
has ended in ruin and public infamy for me, yet
the memory of our ancient affection is often with
me, and the thought that loathing, bitterness and
contempt should for ever take that place in my
heart once held by love is very sad to me: and you
yourself will, I think, feel in your heart that to
write to me as I lie in the loneliness of prison life
is better than to publish my letters without my
permission or to dedicate poems to me unasked,
though the world will know nothing of whatever
words of grief or passion, of remorse or indifference
you may choose to send as your answer or your
appeal.

I have no doubt that in this letter in which I
have to write of your life and of mine, of the past
and of the future, of sweet things changed to
bitterness and of bitter things that may be turned
into joy, there will be much that will wound your
vanity to the quick. If it prove so, read the letter
over and over again till it kills your vanity. If you
find in it something of which you feel that you

are unjustly accused, remember that one should be thankful that there is any fault of which one can be unjustly accused. If there be in it one single passage that brings tears to your eyes, weep as we weep in prison where the day no less than the night is set apart for tears. It is the only thing that can save you. If you go complaining to your mother, as you did with reference to the scorn of you I displayed in my letter to Robbie, so that she may flatter and soothe you back into self-complacency or conceit, you will be completely lost. If you find one false excuse for yourself, you will soon find a hundred, and be just what you were before. Do you still say, as you said to Robbie in your answer, that I *'attribute unworthy motives'* to you? Ah! you had no motives in life. You had appetites merely. A motive is an intellectual aim. That you were *'very young'* when our friendship began? Your defect was not that you knew so little about life, but that you knew so much. The morning dawn of boyhood with its delicate bloom, its clear pure light, its joy of innocence and expectation you had left far behind. With very swift and running feet you had passed from Romance to Realism. The gutter and the things that live in it had begun to fascinate you. That was the origin of the trouble in which you sought my aid, and I, so unwisely according to the wisdom of this world, out of pity and kindness gave it to you. You must read this letter right through, though each word may become to you as the fire or knife of the surgeon that makes the delicate flesh burn or bleed. Remember that the

152

fool in the eyes of the gods and the fool in the eyes of man are very different. One who is entirely ignorant of the modes of Art in its revolution or the moods of thought in its progress, of the pomp of the Latin line or the richer music of the vowelled Greek, of Tuscan sculpture or Elizabethan song may yet be full of the very sweetest wisdom. The real fool, such as the gods mock or mar, is he who does not know himself. I was such a one too long. You have been such a one too long. Be so no more. Do not be afraid. The supreme vice is shallowness. Everything that is realised is right. Remember also that whatever is misery to you to read, is still greater misery to me to set down. To you the Unseen Powers have been very good. They have permitted you to see the strange and tragic shapes of Life as one sees shadows in a crystal. The head of Medusa that turns living men to stone you have been allowed to look at in a mirror merely. You yourself have walked free among the flowers. From me the beautiful world of colour and motion has been taken away.

I will begin by telling you that I blame myself terribly. As I sit here in this dark cell in convict clothes, a disgraced and ruined man, I blame myself. In the perturbed and fitful nights of anguish, in the long monotonous days of pain, it is myself I blame. I blame myself for allowing an unintellectual friendship, a friendship whose primary aim was not the creation and contemplation of beautiful things, to entirely dominate my life. From the very first there was

153

too wide a gap between us. You had been idle at your school, worse than idle at your university. You did not realise that an artist, and especially such an artist as I am, one, that is to say, the quality of whose work depends on the intensification of personality, requires for the development of his art the companionship of ideas, an intellectual atmosphere, quiet, peace and solitude. You admired my work when it was finished: you enjoyed the brilliant successes of my first nights, and the brilliant banquets that followed them: you were proud, and quite naturally so, of being the intimate friend of an artist so distinguished; but you could not understand the conditions requisite for the production of artistic work. I am not speaking in phrases of rhetorical exaggeration but in terms of absolute truth to actual fact when I remind you that during the whole time we were together I never wrote one single line. Whether at Torquay, Goring, London, Florence or elsewhere, my life, as long as you were by my side, was entirely sterile and uncreative. And with but few intervals you were, I regret to say, by my side always.

[. . .]

For yourself, I have but this last thing to say. Do not be afraid of the past. If people tell you that it is irrevocable, do not believe them. The past, the present and the future are but one moment in the sight of God, in whose sight we should try to live. Time and space, succession and extension, are merely accidental conditions of Thought. The Imagination can transcend them

154

and move in a free sphere of ideal existences. Things, also, are in their essence what we choose to make them. A thing *is,* according to the mode in which one looks at it. 'Where others,' says Blake, 'see but the Dawn coming over the hill, I see the sons of God shouting for joy.' What seemed to the world and to myself my future I lost irretrievably when I let myself be taunted into taking the action against your father: had, I dare say, lost it really long before that. What lies before me is my past. I have got to make myself look on that with different eyes, to make the world look on it with different eyes, to make God look on it with different eyes. This I cannot do by ignoring it, or slighting it, or praising it, or denying it. It is only to be done by fully accepting it as an inevitable part of the evolution of my life and character: by bowing my head to everything that I have suffered. How far I am away from the true temper of soul, this letter in its changing, uncertain moods, its scorn and bitterness, its aspirations and its failure to realise those aspirations, shows you quite clearly. But do not forget in what a terrible school I am sitting at my task. And incomplete, imperfect, as I am, yet from me you may have still much to gain. You came to me to learn the Pleasure of Life and the Pleasure of Art. Perhaps I am chosen to teach you something much more wonderful, the meaning of Sorrow, and its beauty.

Your affectionate friend, Oscar Wilde

from *De Profundis*, OSCAR WILDE

Index of Poem Titles

Index of First Lines